4/15

Little Miss MUFFET

Flip-Side Rhymes

From the
perspective of
Little Miss Muffet

by Christopher Harbo

illustrated by Colin Jack

PICTURE WINDOW BOOKS
a capstone imprint

Little Miss Muffet

sat on a tuffet,

eating her curds and whey.

Along came a spider,

who sat down beside her

and frightened
Miss Muffet away.

Little Miss MUFFET

FLip-SIDE Rhymes

From the perspective of the spider

by christopher Harbo

illustrated by colin Jack

PICTURE WINDOW BOOKS
a capstone imprint

The spider spied Muffet

perched on the tuffet,

so he crawled down

to ask her to play.

With a high-pitched squeal,

the girl tossed her meal.

9

Now he's swimming
in curds and whey.

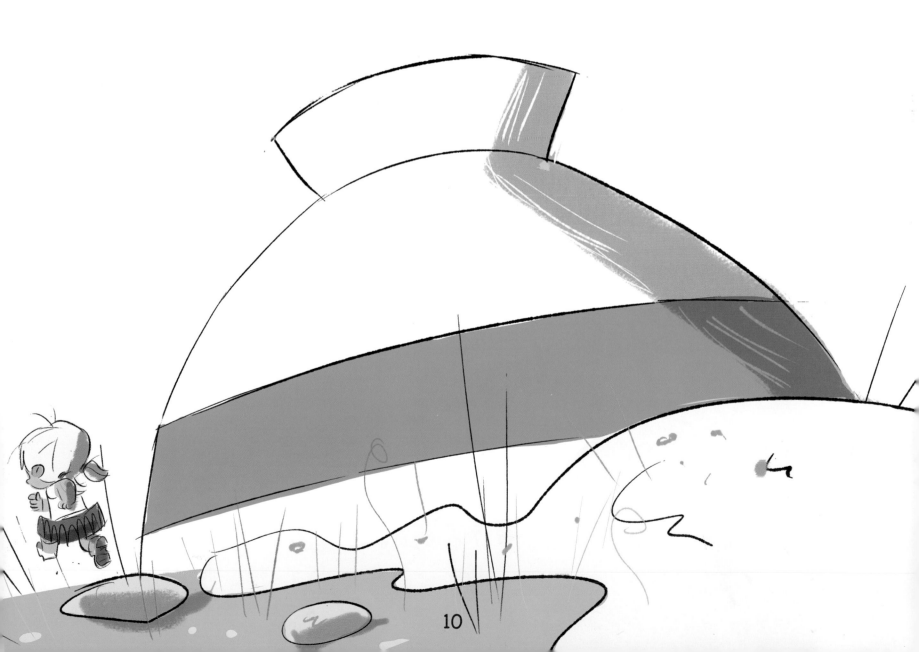

Other titles in this series:

Humpty **DUMPTY**
FLIP-Side Rhymes

JACK and Jill
FLIP-Side Rhymes

Little **BO PEEP**
FLIP-Side Rhymes

NOW FLIP THE BOOK
TO GET ANOTHER SIDE OF THE RHYME.

NOW FLIP THE BOOK
TO GET ANOTHER SIDE OF THE RHYME.

Editor: Gillia Olson
Designer: Ashlee Suker
Art Director: Nathan Gassman
Production Specialist: Laura Manthe
The illustrations in this book were created digitally.

Picture Window Books are published by Capstone.
1710 Roe Crest Drive, North Mankato, Minnesota 56003
www.capstonepub.com

Library of Congress Cataloging-in-Publication Data
Harbo, Christopher L.
Little Miss Muffet flip-side rhymes / by Christopher Harbo ; illustrated by Colin Jack.
    pages cm. — (Nonfiction picture books. Flip-side nursery rhymes)
    Summary: "Color illustrations and simple text give the original Little Miss Muffett
nursery rhyme, along with a fractured version from the perspective of the spider—
Provided by publisher.
    ISBN 978-1-4795-5987-9 (library binding)
    ISBN 978-1-4795-5991-6 (paperback)
    ISBN 978-1-4795-6003-5 (big book)
    ISBN 978-1-4795-6007-3 (paper over board)
    ISBN 978-1-4795-6985-4 (eBook PDF)
    1. Nursery rhymes. 2. Children's poetry. 3. Upside-down books—Specimens.
[1. Nursery rhymes. 2. Upside-down books.] I. Jack, Colin, illustrator. II. Mother
Goose. III. Title.
    PZ8.3.M19669Lk 2015
    398.2—dc23 [E]   2014032218
                                                                008482C6S15

Printed in the United States of America in North Mankato, Minnesota.
092014   008482CS15